HELP! MY BABY DIED

Reggie Weems

Consulting Editor: Dr. Paul Tautges

Help! My Baby Died

ISBN
Paper: 978-1-63342-021-2
epub: 978-1-63342-022-9
Kindle: 978-1-63342-023-6

Published by **Shepherd Press**
P.O. Box 24
Wapwallopen, PA 18660

www.shepherdpress.com

All Scripture quotations, unless stated otherwise, are from the English Standard Version (Crossway, 2001)

All Scripture quotations, unless stated otherwise, are from the English Standard Version (Crossway, 2001)

Designed by **documen**

To

Teana

Contents

INTRODUCTION

The greatest grief any parent can endure is the death of a child. No other human experience compares to it. The death of children seems to reverse the natural order of creation. It awakens us from the slumber of daily existence to the stark reality of a world gone painfully awry. After the birth of our second daughter, Teana and I wept over the loss of three children we have yet to meet; each bereavement compounded by the previous trauma, a seemingly endless nightmare. The weakness felt by a mother who cannot rescue a dying child is multiplied for a father who helplessly walks alongside his wife, unable to save his child from death or his wife from heartache.

As a husband and son-in-law, I had stood with Teana and her parents as her nine-year-old brother, who had Down syndrome, exhaled his final breath. In the aftermath of Jimmy's unexpected death, Teana whispered to me, "I will never smile again."

As a pastor, I have watched parents struggle vainly to breathe on behalf of children dependent on life-support systems; listened to mothers and fathers present their own lives to God in exchange for their child's life, or offer a doctor their own hearts, kidneys, or lungs in exchange for the failing organs of a baby; and sat in innumerable living rooms as parents poured out questions like tears. As a friend, I have walked away from cemeteries with parents whose hearts remained mesmerized by a shoebox-sized casket solemnly lowered out of sight and deep into a ground that maliciously swallowed their hope, joy, and future.

In such moments of inexpressible grief we wonder how the planet could continue spinning; how people could go on living as though the whole world had not been irreparably broken. It seems that human decency would demand that everyone hide along the funeral route. There are few things more perplexing than traveling behind a hearse, watching cars and people go about their daily business, and questioning why everyone hasn't fallen under the weight of such grief. But no one on earth can fully identify with your sorrow and you can't make anyone understand.

Teana's brother Jimmy was born with an inoperable congenital heart defect. He died unexpectedly of a heart attack as the family enjoyed a ride on an amusement train in Blowing Rock, North Carolina, approximately two hours from his parents' home. He had seen commercials for the train on television and the one-day vacation was an answer to his ongoing pleas to visit the amusement park. On the way home from the emergency room in nearby Boone, the funeral home hearse passed us going in the opposite direction on its way to retrieve Jimmy's body. The family inhaled deeply as the two cars slowly passed each other on the narrow, winding mountain road. Many families will not fully exhale until they are reunited with children in heaven.

The death of a child is a unique experience; the shadow of a deep, darkened valley through which some families sorrowfully pass. Words are insufficient to describe the emotion. Pictures cannot adequately capture the moments. The inexpressible loss can be only partially described but never fully defined. It is a waiting—for it not to be true and then, once no longer denied, for it to be made untrue—and then a moment-by-moment longing for time itself to end so that it will seem to have never been true.

Until that time, this book is offered as encouragement from one fellow sufferer to another. It is intended to be brief and thus will not answer every question about your experience or your baby. But it does answer one very important question: there is indeed a God, and he is faithful and worthy of your trust, even now—especially now. He is the eternal, inextinguishable hope for grieving families. If in the process of reading this book you arrive at that realization for the first time, I will rejoice that others have gained a reprieving breath from the most traumatic sorrow any parent can endure.

But what! Do you think her lost, when she is
but sleeping in the bosom of the Almighty!
Think not her absent who is in such a friend's house.
Is she lost to you who is found to Christ?

Samuel Rutherford[1]

1 How Can You Mend a Broken Heart?

There are momentous occasions we all choose to remember: our wedding day, the birth of a child, or a visit to an exotic destination. Memories are our imagination at work over the past, the pictures that recall the wonder, even the worth of our lives; the gateways to other times and places while we remain confined to the present. There are occasions of personal significance to my family during which Teana will say, "I'm freezing this moment to remember forever." But not all memories are prized as treasures worth keeping.

The ability to remember is both a blessing and a bane. Memories keep us from harm by reminding us of unpleasant experiences we need to avoid in the future. As a child I endured a torturous sunburn on the coast of Barcelona, Spain, and, as a result, my wife and children have laughed ever since about my extreme devotion to shade at the beach. And more than once I have scolded my children for their lack of appreciation for suntan lotion.

While I only remember events of either immense positive or negative significance, Teana remembers everything. Of course, this has its positive and negative aspects for a husband. My first full memory is of when, at the age of eleven, I first met Teana in Athens, Greece. That's where my life began. She, on the other hand, has an uncanny ability to recall events when she was two years old. So it is no wonder that, when I wanted to tell the story of our loss, Teana served as my navigator, compass, and North Star. Our discussions reanimated tears long since shed as she graciously and patiently recounted details of each trauma, many particulars of which I was unaware, had forgotten, or had subliminally stricken from memory in self-preservation.

Before our marriage, doctors informed Teana that it would be improbable that she would conceive children. At the time it was of little consequence to me, for she was prize enough to fill my whole world with room for little else. As a young married couple, life was an adventure expressed by our first home, Pacific Grove, California, the land of butterflies, whale sightings, deer in the back yard, long walks along a nearby beach, and all the kaleidoscope of variety afforded by what the locals called "PG" and nearby Carmel, Monterey, and San Francisco.

With the doctor's prognosis ringing in our ears, it was to our surprise and immense delight that Teana delivered our first child, Stephanie René, in December 1978 without any complications (except, perhaps, for the thirty-two hours of very active and hard labor). Two days shy of two years later, Angela Hope was born into our family. In addition, Teana was in labor with our second child for only about six hours. In the midst of our joy, however, Teana longed for a son. She read the Bible stories of Hannah and her son Samuel with amazement and an accompanying prayer that God would likewise bless her with a son. She, like Hannah, even dedicated this yet-to-be-born child to God. And, with two perfect children in our lives, every reason existed for optimism. But if unexpected and overwhelming joy had been the undergirding tone of our lives to that date, it was soon to be replaced with music in minor keys that seemed destined to repeat itself again and again.

Three years later, on the Friday before Mother's Day, Teana visited a local restaurant as the guest speaker at a banquet honoring the mothers of our city. As an expectant mother, and already the mother of two perfect daughters, we both looked forward to our next child as the particular answer to her unceasing prayers. As Teana enjoyed the meal and conversation that evening with other women, however, she felt her chair moistening. Excusing herself to the restroom, she discovered that she was bleeding.[2] She remained throughout the banquet, fulfilled her calling to share a word of encouragement to the mothers present, and then returned home to rejoin our little family. Once home, she called the doctor and explained her condition and the surrounding circumstances. The physician initially placed Teana on bed rest. He called in a prescription, which I retrieved from the pharmacy, and encouraged her to wait until morning to contact him again.

Teana remained in bed all day Saturday as the girls and I waited on her every need, leaving her to rest in the hopeful anticipation that sleep would help pass the time and ease her anxiety. By evening neither the bleeding nor her pain had subsided, so she and I made our way to the local hospital. Later that evening, the day before Mother's Day 1983, Teana suffered her first miscarriage in the local hospital emergency room. As she was still in her first trimester, the baby was small enough for the doctor to place in a sterile cup. Later, as he explained what had happened, we heard the words "spontaneous abortion," a phrase that sickened our hearts and raised many unanswered questions.

"Horror" is an insufficient word to describe the sudden and permanent reversal of everything we had hoped. Yet in spite of her sorrow, Teana remained so firm in the expectation of a son that her faith generated persevering strength toward the thought of another pregnancy. Incredibly, she was once again expecting another child the very next year. In May 1984 she was one week shy of her second trimester when she began experiencing severe cramps. Her pain began over the weekend and doctors advised her to wait until Monday before proceeding to the office or, if necessary, to emergency care. The weekend became our waiting room as we cried and prayed while attempting to maintain the smiling faces of hope before one another and our daughters.

On that Monday an ultrasound scan in the doctor's office revealed that the baby was not growing in her womb. Teana was enduring pain caused by an ectopic pregnancy. I vividly remember standing in the elevator with Teana as we left the doctor's office. We were joined by one other passenger who, I am sure, wondered at the young couple whose tear-stained faces turned toward the exterior of that small cubicle and leaned in unison against its walls for any sense of support.

At the hospital, my wife was immediately

ushered into an operating room where she endured emergency surgery. Much to the amazement of the surgeon and Teana's personal physician, the baby had been growing in her ovary and not in her fallopian tube. Still, one ovary and the accompanying fallopian tube, as well as the baby, were removed during surgery. Our doctor attempted to assure us that the baby could not have survived outside the womb, but the manner in which our child died still haunted us. And there was more to come.

A pregnancy test administered after Teana's surgery revealed that she was still pregnant. One of her physicians suspected that Teana had been carrying twins and that one baby was still alive. Could it be that optimism was warranted? In spite of the news, we attempted to place any expectation on hold with skepticism as the counterbalance to hope. Our suspicion was proven true later that very same day when another doctor informed us that the pregnancy test was most assuredly a false positive resulting from hormones still present in Teana's body from the ectopic pregnancy. And so Teana remained in the hospital for a few days, recovering from surgery and the loss of another baby.

My most poignant memory of the loss of our second child was the pain I felt for Teana as we left the doctor's office after the initial diagnosis. I simply could not endure her further pain. In the elevator I leaned against my wife and whispered, "We can't do this anymore, Baby." Yet unbeknownst to us, we were far from the end of our travail.

One year later to the very month, Teana was enjoying her second trimester of another pregnancy with an uneasiness born of experience. She had already chosen boy and girl names for the baby but was nonetheless fearful of another miscarriage. On one particular occasion, a well-meaning friend attempted to encourage her with the words "God is good, and he will not let this happen to you again." I've heard it said that if you want to make God laugh, tell him your plans.

Only a few days later, late one evening, Teana began bleeding. She called the doctor but he reassured her that the experience was not uncommon during pregnancy. He encouraged her to sleep and see if anything further transpired overnight. But the next morning's arrival only furthered her concerns with heavier bleeding. At the doctor's office that morning an ultrasound revealed that the baby didn't have a heartbeat. The physician encouraged us to return home and wait until Teana naturally delivered the baby. Feeling some internal pressure, Teana excused herself to the restroom where her bleeding increased and cramps began. At that point Teana recognized that she was in labor and called for the nurse, who informed the doctor of what was occurring.

The physician's office was located on the premises of the hospital and he personally escorted us as I pushed Teana down a long corridor toward a glass window partitioning the hallway from the hospital cafeteria. Just as we neared the window Teana looked down to see that her bleeding covered the wheelchair seat. Blood had begun to seep up the light green dress she was wearing, on her side against the window and evident to anyone looking in her direction. It was the longest walk of our lives as I cautiously wheeled her away from the doctor's office, down the hallway, up an elevator, on to a hospital floor, and into a bed where she delivered her third breathless child. Shortly afterwards, Teana was taken to an operating room, where the doctor and a team of associates ministered to her bleeding.

How is it possible to love and miss someone you've never met? For the third time in three years, my wife's heart was broken by unrealized hope, and my heart was broken for the loss of children and for her. Love moved her heart to believe and to try, but she experienced a pain that almost equaled in strength her desire for children. Where can broken people turn to in such times of unexpected, repetitive, seemingly senseless and deep sorrow? Thankfully we did not have to look far. Teana and I found refuge in an ancient piece of wisdom literature.

2 Children, Sin, and Death

What Teana and I needed most was rhyme and reason. Was there a poetic end to the pain we endured, perhaps an overarching scheme that would provide such a sufficient explanation that at some point we could look at each other and say, "It was worth it"? Was there a single answer so sufficient that some questions could remain unanswered?

Specifically, Teana and I both asked ourselves a multiplied number of times, "What happens to babies when they die?" It seemed that if this question could legitimately be answered it would serve as a rainbow after the storm. It could provide the hopeful promise of a purpose and plan that might not altogether explain the "why" of our exact losses but would nonetheless inspire hope for the future. Yet somehow we both also knew that, apart from a divinely inspired word, a word if you will, of revelation, this single most important question could not be answered with soul-satisfying certainty.

Neither of us was raised in an overtly religious home, but in the aftermath of our surreal, almost ethereal experiences, we surmised that the Christian God could speak definitively with regard to an infant's well-being after death. And so it was that in Christianity we discovered answers that speak so caringly and sufficiently to any parent whose child dies. Simply put, the Bible offered us the best answer, a comforting answer, and the really only sufficient answer on which any family can rest the hope of reunion with children who have preceded them in death. That answer, however, begins not at the end of life but at its beginning.

A Sinful Conception

Christians believe that life begins at conception, but this conviction leads to questions about the souls of children who die. There are a lot of different perspectives on the subject, even among Christians. Yet our unease does not present a difficulty for God. One reason for legitimate concern is that the Bible clearly teaches that every human being after Adam, the first man, is conceived in sin and separated from God. God warned our first parents, Adam and Eve, that defiance against his Word would result in death, and it did, death becoming a natural part of life. As Adam's descendants, all human beings are born spiritually dead, separated from God, unable to reconcile themselves to him, as children of wrath, and wholly dependent on his beneficent grace. Teaching about Adam's fall and its consequences in Romans 5:12, the apostle Paul wrote, "sin came into the world through one man, and death through sin." Even the great King David, the "man after God's own heart," penned, "I was brought forth in iniquity, and in sin did my mother conceive me" (Psalm 51:5). In reality, this is the condition of every human being ever born or who will ever be born.[3] All people are conceived and born as sinners, are naturally separated from God at birth, and are dependent on God's unmerited favor from the moment of conception.

Thus, despite appearances, babies are conceived and born as sinners. From the moment of their conception, each one of them carried our sinful DNA. There is simply no biblical way to avoid this reality. Children, like adults, die as a result of their connection to the human race. This occurs even though children may die before committing any actual sin, proving that death is simply the result of our association with Adam. The universality of death proves the universality of sinfulness. If children were not sinners, no child would ever die. However, the Bible is clear that God is a God of grace. Just as the good news of the Bible is that, through Christ, we can find mercy and forgiveness for our sins and be reconciled to God, so there are also clear examples in the Bible of God showing mercy in judgment to adults and children who could not discern right from wrong. In Deuteronomy 1:39, God specifically exempted those who had "no knowledge of good or evil" from the punishment inflicted on adults who had received his Word and volitionally rebelled against him. The Lord later asked Jonah, "should not I pity Nineveh, that great city, in which there are more than 120,000 persons who do not know their right hand from their left . . .?" (Jonah 4:11), a possible reference to infants, children, or others who were incapable of judging right from wrong. God extends mercy to every person who does not possess the mental faculties to comprehend him or to be convicted by the Holy Spirit of God's right eous standard, personal sin, or its consequential judgment. Certainly, such precious children and adults are considered as infants before the Lord. They are sinners by nature, yet in his grace God does not eternally banish them from his presence.

Yet, it is not because a child is innocent—no child is—but because of God's mercy that he saves (Titus 3:5). John McArthur writes,

> *All children who die before they reach the state of moral awareness and culpability, in which they understand their sin and corruption—so that their sins are deliberate—are graciously saved eternally by God through the work of Jesus Christ. They are counted as elect by sovereign choice because they are innocent of willful sin, rebellion, and unbelief, by which works they would be justly condemned to eternal punishment.*[4]

When our three living children were toddlers, Teana began teaching them the Ten Commandments. This is because Paul confessed, "through the law comes knowledge of sin" (Romans 3:20) and we wanted the children to know Christ at an early age. The Law presents God's holy character, pricks the human conscience, proves our condemnation, and points us to Christ: "the law was our guardian until Christ came, in order that we might be justified by faith" (Galatians 3:24). But what about children who never understand the concept of sin, who are unable to conceptualize righteousness, and who cannot comprehend the necessity for or the availability of salvation? Unlike our living children's ability to comprehend sin, the gospel, or God's existence, Teana's nine-year-old brother, Jimmy, never understood these concepts. The severity of his Down syndrome proved to be the circumstance by which his parents became Christians, but he never comprehended the great blessing God orchestrated through his life.

In the Bible, Teana and I began to find an answer to the most important question that faced us during our losses: "Would we ever meet the children conceived yet lost to us?" A host of scriptural references seemed to point us in a direction of trust in the God who not only created our children but also oversaw all creation.

3 God Is Not Silent

Fortunately, parents do not stare at a blank page when consulting the Scriptures concerning conception, birth, life, and death. This is important, for many children do not escape the ultimate cost of living in a fallen world. In his biography of American theologian Jonathan Edwards, George Marsden comments that an early 18th-century American children's prayer included the words, "Lord, if my Soul this night take / Let me by morning then in Heav'n wake."[5] Our modern version is spoken as, "Now I lay me down to sleep, / I pray the Lord my soul to keep. / If I should die before I wake, / I pray the Lord my soul to take." In Edwards' era the prayer was a sincere, if not desperate, Godward plea from Christians who lived in circumstances that daily threatened the survival of adults and children alike.

Although seldom acknowledged, life is equally frail in the 21st century. That 18th-century sense of daily dread has been minimized by medical technology but it has not been altogether eliminated. This is evidenced by the life and death of Kari Schoondyke. Kari was born in 2008 with a congenital heart defect discovered by her dad, a cardiologist, shortly after Kari arrived home from the hospital. She endured her first surgery at nine days old but required a second surgery, from which she did not recover. Kari died before her seven-month birthday. Many years after our own losses, the study for this particular book was actually occasioned by Kari's death and the sincere desire to offer comfort and hope to hurting friends, parents, and families.

Many of the answers Teana and I discovered to questions about the life and death of children are found in the book of Psalms, located almost in the middle of the Christian Bible. There we read that God numbers the days of every person ever conceived. David wrote,

> . . . *in your book were written, every one of them,*
> *the days that were formed for me,*
> *when as yet there was none of them.*
> (Psalm 139:16)

It was an amazing revelation to learn that God, not circumstance or happenstance, determines the life span of every human being. Even before any of our six children were conceived God had already determined their life spans. This psalm informs us that, in spite of modern scientific claims or medical advances, length-of-life issues are not ultimately decided by anyone other than God, who, in his impeccable wisdom, begins and ends life. He and he alone saw our children's "unformed substance" and wrote down the days he would allot to them (v. 16).

The God about whom we were learning is the God who hems in our lives like a woven garment, "behind [after death] and before [before conception]," and whose hand is ever on us (v. 5). He's even present in the womb, "intricately" weaving children together as he sees fit (v. 15). From this psalm, Teana and I learned that children are a gift from the God who controls everything, who knits babies together and forms their every part (v. 13). David likened his life to a garment that God divinely sewed together knowing all of its ins and outs; how he would begin it, and the day and manner in which it would be finished. He then summarized his thought processes in verse 6 by announcing that such a plan was too wonderful for him to understand. And so it is for you and me.

After surveying the sovereignty of God over all of life, David concluded,

> *I praise you, for I am fearfully and*
> *wonderfully made.*
> *Wonderful are your works;*
> *my soul knows it very well.*
>
> (v. 14)

This truth about God's providence in the lives of children is echoed in other Bible verses as well. When, in the Old Testament, Job heard that his children had unexpectedly died, he correctly exclaimed,

> *The Lord gave, and the Lord has taken away.*
>
> (*Job* 1:21)

In the New Testament, Jesus's claim to the title of "Alpha and . . . Omega, the beginning and the end" (Revelation 21:6) implies everything, even life itself. This is an amazing comfort to people who know God and believe that he always does what is morally right as well as what is in the best interests of his people, including children not yet born, infants, toddlers, and those mentally unable to receive or reject Christ.

Eventually, Teana and I learned that the Bible does not have all the answers for every individual situation or particular question. It does not explain everything we want to know about God's plan or even tell us that we would understand that plan if God did reveal it. But God revealed himself in Jesus Christ in such a way as to be *the* ultimate Answer to everything. How wonderful to know that a great and gracious God was with all our children at the very beginning of life and most assuredly cared for three of them as they entered his never-dying presence!

God Opens and Shuts the Womb

The Bible is clear that it is God who gives women the ability to conceive children. The word translated "womb" occurs for the first time in the Bible in the midst of a startling declaration that "the LORD had closed all the wombs of the house of Abimelech" (Genesis 20:18). By this assertion, the Lord unequivocally demonstrated his authority over conception. The very next reference to the womb is in like fashion but with a very different outcome; Moses wrote in Genesis 29:31, "When the LORD saw that Leah was hated, he opened her womb, but Rachel was barren." In retrospect, but under divine inspiration, Moses acknowledged that God opened Leah's womb and, by implication, led his readers to understand that Rachel was barren at God's discretion. The "why" of such circumstances is a dark mystery beyond human comprehension, but the Author of such circumstances is certainly knowable and equally trustworthy.

The Hebrew patriarchs understood God's sovereign control over life and death. Green with envy toward Leah, and desperate in the race against her sister for their husband Jacob's love, Rachel cried out to him, "Give me children, or I shall die!" In response, "Jacob's anger was kindled against Rachel, and he said, "Am I in the place of God, who has withheld from you the fruit of the womb?" (Genesis 30:1–2). As the grandson of a miraculous conception, Jacob knew that the ability to conceive a child lay with God and not human beings. In his perfect timing, and for his eternal purposes, God eventually "remembered Rachel, and . . . listened to her and opened her womb" (Genesis 30:22). Just before his death, Jacob instilled the knowledge of God's sovereignty in his children, giving praise to "the Almighty who will bless you with blessings of heaven above, blessings of the deep that crouches beneath, blessings of the breasts and of the womb" (Genesis 49:25).

Back in the 139th psalm, David exclaimed in

verse 13, "you formed my inward parts; you knitted me together in my mother's womb." Isaiah also declared that God "formed you from the womb" (Isaiah 44:2). Time and again, the Old Testament reveals how God's people viewed the conception and birth of children. Amazingly, God is not only involved at the beginning of life but throughout, and most assuredly at its end.

God Graciously Works in the Lives of Children in the Womb

In the-18th-century hymn "Amazing Grace," John Newton wrote, "His word my hope secures," and so it does. But is there any scriptural evidence that God works spiritually while children are still in the womb? Thankfully, the Bible does speak of God's perspective on babies and his gracious work in the lives of unborn infants and even children too.

For instance, the Bible calls Moses a "fine child" at birth (Exodus 2:2). The Hebrew word translated "fine" ranges anywhere from physical beauty to moral uprightness. But in Acts 7:20, Stephen interpreted the words "a fine child" as "beautiful in God's sight." Moses was born a sinner and as an adult he became a murderer, but at birth he was beautiful in God's sight. Isaac also experienced God's gracious providence before his birth. Before he was born, God told Isaac's father, Abraham, "Sarah your wife shall bear you a son, and you shall call his name Isaac. I will establish my covenant with him as an everlasting covenant for his offspring after him . . . I will establish my covenant with Isaac . . ." (Genesis 17:19, 21). For God to establish his covenant with Isaac even before he was born, Isaac must have been elect of the Lord, a subject of God's grace before his conception, in the womb and then as a growing child.

David's first child died soon after its birth. During the baby's illness David fasted, wept, and prayed to God on the child's behalf. His demeanor changed, however, after the child's death. He bathed, put on clean clothes, and went to the temple to worship God. In response to apparent concern that David was not properly mourning, he replied, "While the child was still alive, I fasted and wept, for I said, 'Who knows whether the LORD will be gracious to me, that the child may live?' But now he is dead. Why should I fast? Can I bring him back again? I shall go to him, but he will not return to me" (2 Samuel 12:22–23). David's comment "I shall go to him" assured his court of his perspective on his child's death; he certainly didn't have the grave in mind. Rather, David understood God's grace to be sufficient for his baby. Once the child died he focused his attention on a reunion with his baby, a thought that enabled him to face life with joy.

Luke, the Gospel writer, implied that John the Baptist knew God in the womb when he wrote, “he will be filled with the Holy Spirit, even from his mother’s womb” (Luke 1:15). His mother, Elizabeth, confirmed this when she stated, “the baby in my womb leaped for joy” (Luke 1:44) upon hearing Mary’s announcement concerning her pregnancy with Jesus. Finally, in concert with his Old Testament predecessors, the apostle Paul was both “set . . . apart” and “called . . . by . . . grace” while still in the womb (Galatians 1:15–16).

News of God’s redeeming work in the lives of children who are not yet born certainly brought comfort to Teana and me. Then again, how could we expect any less from our God? He created us, and even when we rebelled against him, he pursued us with an unwavering passion. If he deals so graciously with sinners who actively participate in mutiny against him, how much kinder will he be toward those who are born sinners by virtue of their relationship to Adam but who have not personally sinned against him, dying with no awareness of his holiness, subsequent wrath, or possible salvation?

The Bible reveals that God does work spiritually in the lives of children, even in the womb. There is no reason why God could not save any child before its birth or thereafter. There is therefore every reason to believe that children who die before birth, while in infancy, or before the age of spiritual awareness are in heaven.

The Golden Chain of Salvation

In Romans 8, Paul outlines God's program of salvation. He writes, "For those whom he foreknew he also predestined to be conformed to the image of his Son, in order that he might be the firstborn among many brothers. And those whom he predestined he also called, and those whom he called he also justified, and those whom he justified he also glorified" (vv. 29–30). Basically, every person who is ever glorified (going to heaven) is also justified (made right with God), called (selected), predestined (chosen), and foreknown (known beforehand). No one goes to heaven apart from what is often called "the golden chain of salvation."

Interestingly, every act of God in the salvation process of Romans 8 (foreknowledge, predestination, calling, justification, and glorification) can also be divinely bestowed on infants, babies, and young children. It must be remembered that Christ's death is the actual basis of any person's salvation. This is why the apostle Paul taught that people are saved only by grace yet through faith. It is grace that saves, not the act of human faith. So it is quite possible for God to call and justify babies in the womb or soon after birth, since this is the same way God saves all people. As in many of the scriptural examples I've presented, God can and does awaken infants who then respond to Christ, whether in the womb or after birth. He does this in the same way he awakens adults who are spiritually dead in sin and unaware of God. So the grace that saved Teana and me is the same grace that has saved our adult children and could save the babies whom we have yet to meet.

In reality, then, adults are in the same situation as children, wholly dependent on God's grace. Unsaved adults are as ignorant of God as a baby in the womb; as unaware of Christ as a recently born child; and as unable to trust in Christ as a baby who has never seen the light of day or an infant who does not yet have the capacity to formulate constructive thought. Fundamentally, it is no more difficult or different for God to save a baby than it is for him to save a spiritually dead adult.

God's grace is all the more visibly magnified through saving babies who are so evidently dependent on his grace. In other words, the saving of infants demonstrates precisely how God saves any adult who repents of sin and believes on Jesus Christ. It is perhaps for this very reason that the Lord Jesus highlighted children as natural recipients of his saving grace. In Matthew 18:3, he states, "Truly, I say to you, unless you turn and become like children, you will never enter the kingdom of heaven." In Matthew 19:14, Jesus says, "Let the little children come to me and do not hinder them, for to such belongs the kingdom of heaven." The salvation of infants is a perfect illustration of God's grace at work. It reminds us of how dependent upon God every person is for salvation. Children don't have any works to condemn them before God. Yet neither do they have any works to commend them to God. For this reason, the salvation of infants is in perfect harmony with the grace that saves every person who repents of personal sin and trusts in Jesus Christ. Have you?

The gospel is the good news that Jesus died for sinners like you and me, and rose from the dead. The Bible assures us that we who turn from our sin, and place our faith in Jesus Christ as Savior and Lord, enter into a personal relationship with God that gives us divine life now and secures our well-being for eternity. Do you recognize your own sinfulness, and see God's wrath against sin? Have you trusted in Jesus alone as the only and full remedy for it? Will you call out to him in faith, believing that he saves all who do so? Jesus himself says, "Repent and believe" (Mark 1:15), and "Come to me" (Matthew 11:28).

4 A Well-Placed Hope

Understanding the salvation of infants not only offered comfort to Teana and me, it can also offer hope to your grieving family. In his eternal, all-knowing counsel, God considered every circumstance that might occur in human history and included it in a single, unified plan of salvation that was fully accomplished when Jesus was crucified at Calvary, and rose from the grave three days later. As benefactors of that unmerited grace, we witness God's greatness in his graciousness toward infants. As such, he is our well-placed hope, the eternal, inextinguishable hope of which I spoke in the Introduction to this book.

For this reason, Teana and I ultimately discovered that the real answer to our sorrow and seemingly insurmountable hopelessness was not in the eternal welfare of any of our children who died, or even in answers the Scriptures provided, but in God alone.

It is not uncommon for people to read the Bible thinking that its primary purpose is to make sense of life. Surely, people think there is a verse to answer every question, a reference for every hurt. The desire for answers is all the more accentuated by sorrow. Anguish can be multiplied in the incalculable expanse between finite knowledge and infinite wisdom. Yet possessing truth does not always imply finding satisfaction. And misapplied truth is as fatal as a lie. In the process, we deny ourselves God's important purpose in the divine revelation of the Bible.

Rather than being a manifesto on the human condition or providing answers about it, the Bible reveals a God who alone can cleanse the human stain, remedy the repercussions of the fall, and satisfy the human heart. The Scriptures teach that Jesus is both the wisdom and the power of God (1 Corinthians 1:24). Scripture therefore has value beyond what you and I seek in it or derive from it. In Scripture, God has revealed himself as he deems appropriate. In that regard, ultimate truth is not so much lessons learned or questions answered, as a Person to be known. Knowing God is, according to Jesus, what eternal and abundant life is all about (John 17:3). In this way, suffering is often God's effective means of bringing us to the end of ourselves and the beginning of a relationship with him.

It may not seem possible to you now, but this current sadness will subside, only to be replaced by another grief, for sorrow is enduring in this lifetime. This again reminds us that our greatest hope is not in the lives of our children or a rescue from heartache, but in God himself, who is more than sufficient throughout all of life and for eternity. This mini-book's primary purpose is, therefore, to inspire the confidence in God for you to say with Teana and me, "Wonderful are your works; my soul knows it very well" (Psalm 139:14). It is written to increase your awe of, hope in, and submission to this great God who has revealed himself in the Bible. His goodness and faithfulness certainly warrant our love and trust.

Several months before I wrote this book, Teana, who ministers as a Registered Nurse in our local hospital, and a co-worker were discussing the suffering of a particular patient and his family. At the end of her account, the co-worker relayed her own sorrow and then, referring to the human grief common to us all, asked Teana, "So what's your story?" Your story of sorrow and grief may have brought this little book to your attention, but its most important benefit will be the personal knowledge of God that you gain while reading. After all, he is the Key to hope, the Anchor of rest, and the Author and Finisher of your salvation and the salvation of your baby.

The Eternal Holiday at God's Sea

In loving grace, yet for reasons still unknown to those of us who remain, God sometimes sees fit to rescue children from the pain of living in a sin-cursed world and receives them to himself. John Newton, from whose hymn "Amazing Grace" I earlier quoted, once wrote to friends, "I hope you are both well reconciled to the death of your child. I cannot be sorry for the death of infants. How many storms do they escape!"[6]

Our hope of being reunited with children who have preceded us to heaven has every scriptural basis, making it a definite hope. Their absence on earth makes heaven even more appealing and our anticipation of heaven all the more passionate. But for all the happiness this thought creates, it is not the real cure for our sorrow. Amid the concepts and words presented in this book is the deep underlying expectation that God will overwhelm you with himself. God himself is the Christian's ultimate hope in and about everything. In our modern world it is easy to talk about God, to be satisfied with the things that are peripheral to him—church attendance, book studies, religious language—but still not know or experience God himself. Yet the best news is not about the benefits God provides but about God himself. Blessings are temporal and of God's sovereign choice, but he always remains, and remains the same.

Modern Christianity often presents God as a means to an end, but this is a poor, self-centered view. God is not a means to an end; he is his own end, and means for us to know him as such. Our souls are so small without him, yet we often substitute something of lesser importance and value for him who alone can satisfy our souls. C. S. Lewis said it like this:

> *Indeed, if we consider the unblushing promises of reward and the staggering nature of the rewards promised in the Gospels, it would seem that Our Lord finds our desire, not too strong, but too weak. We are half-hearted creatures, fooling about . . . when infinite joy is offered us, like an ignorant child who wants to go on making mud pies in a slum because he cannot imagine what is meant by the offer of a holiday at the sea. We are far too easily pleased.*[7]

If nothing else, this book is an encouragement to you to recognize the infinite joy of the eternal holiday by God's sea. Only Jesus can heal the hurt you feel. Only Christ can satisfy the yearning in your soul. Only God's Son can give meaning to your experience and provide hope in the midst of it. And only he can get you out of bed in the morning, help you concentrate on the day's activities, provide tireless strength for the day, and give you inexplicable rest at night. I've witnessed this in the life of my wife and in the lives of a multitude of others who also trust in God.

I've heard it said that time heals all wounds. But I firmly believe that the only time that will heal this wound will be the first time you see God face to face. Still, your sorrow will only be compounded if you endure this earthly tragedy and miss God in the process. More than anything else, I trust this mini-book has directed your heart toward him, and that through it you have found him to be a loving, faithful God; faithful to himself, his Word and his creation.

It may be that you are reading this book as a non-Christian seeking comfort after the death of a child. Nineteenth-century British pastor Charles Spurgeon once addressed the unconverted mothers and fathers of children who had died, saying,

> *Now, let every mother and father here present know assuredly that it is well with the child, if God hath taken it away from you in its infant days . . . Many of you are parents who have children in heaven. Is it not a desirable thing that you should go there, too? . . . Mother, unconverted mother, from the battlements of heaven your child beckons you to Paradise. Father, ungodly, impenitent father, the little eyes that once looked joyously on you, look down upon you now, and the lips which scarcely learned to call you father, ere they were sealed by the silence of death, may be heard as with a still small voice, saying to you this morning, "Father, must we be forever divided by the great gulf which no man can pass?" Doth not nature itself put a sort of longing in your soul that you may be bound in the bundle of life with your own children?*[8]

It is certainly my prayer that you will trust Jesus Christ as your Savior, understanding that "God's kindness is meant to lead you to repentance" (Romans 2:4).

Finally, there is certainly much comfort to be received from those who have preceded us in the loss of children, as they live out the sharing of God's comfort with others.

> *Blessed be the God and Father of our Lord Jesus Christ, the Father of mercies and God of all comfort, who comforts us in all our affliction, so that we may be able to comfort those who are in any affliction, with the comfort with which we ourselves are comforted by God.*
>
> (*2 Corinthians 1:3-4*)

There is much comfort to be received from others, as they live out 2 Corinthians 1:3–4, sharing God's comfort with us. Perhaps this book has been such an expression of God's grace to you. The writings of the Scottish theologian and pastor Samuel Rutherford (1600–1661), whom I quoted in the Introduction, have been such a gift to me. Eight of Rutherford's nine children and his first wife preceded him in death. The political climate of his day banished him from his church for two years, during which he continued his pastoral ministry through letters which were eventually combined into two books titled *A Selection from His Letters by Samuel Rutherford* and *Letters of Samuel Rutherford.* I heartily recommend these books to you as a part of God's healing grace to your soul. Several letters in each book were sent to women grieving the loss of children. In the cold Scottish winter of January 1629, Rutherford penned these words to one suffering congregant:

> *Ye have lost a child: nay she is not lost to you who is found to Christ. She is not sent away, but only sent before, like unto a star, which going out of our sight doth not die and vanish, but shineth in another hemisphere. We see her not, yet she doth shine in another country. If her glass was but a short hour, what she wanteth of time that she hath gotten of eternity; and ye have to rejoice that ye have now some plenishing [furnishings, i.e. home] up in heaven.*[9]

At the very beginning of this book I promised brevity so that you would not have to wade through an encyclopedia to find hope, meaning, rest, and direction. I hope that it has pointed you to our God who alone is worthy of devotion and trust. Between now and the time when we see Jesus revealed in his glory, may "the grace of our Lord Jesus Christ be with you" (1 Thessalonians 5:28).

Conclusion

At some time in the future you will again smile, laugh, and be lighthearted. Teana did. Fifteen years after Jimmy's death her dad also died unexpectedly, but not before he repented of his own sins and trusted Jesus, as did every person in her family, each person influenced by God's work in her brother's illness and death. In the interim, and after three miscarriages, Teana gave birth to our only son and her miracle child, Jonathan David, on our eleventh anniversary. As he omnisciently deems appropriate and in ways presently unforeseen, God will also grant you his grace and unspeakable joy. Sin and suffering simply cannot match God's overwhelming goodness and overcoming grace.

If one word summarizes God's intent in human history it is "promise." Promise is the unifying theme of the Old and New Testaments as God reveals himself to be *the* God who promises and fulfills his word with all of it centering on Jesus Christ. The Old Testament proves his promise unstoppable, and the New Testament proves his promise is ongoing, as the mystery of God's plan unveils itself. Time and again in the Old Testament the prophets and Israel wondered how God would keep his word in the face of seemingly insurmountable odds. But, every time, God proved that it was he and not circumstances or people who were in control of heaven and earth. The resurrection of Jesus Christ became the central proof of God's providential sovereignty. By it he proved that not even death could keep God from fulfilling his promises and so it is with your son or daughter.

A young boy who cannot gain the attention of his parents may, with his hand, reach out and turn his mother or father's face around towards what he is doing as he gleefully exclaims, "Watch this, Mommy" or "Watch this, Daddy." The apostle Paul's defense of the gospel before King Agrippa was that God had not performed his mighty works in a remote corner of the world where no one was watching (Acts 26:26), but had used the entire world, all of creation, as his stage. The Bible and the record of human history are God exclaiming, "Watch this, child. Watch this," as undeniable proof that God keeps his word and is worthy of your trust. As does all the Bible, the saints of Hebrews 11 witness to God's great sufficiency in their lives, no matter this comparatively light, momentary affliction. It is on the basis of that all-sufficient grace that we are encouraged to live with patient endurance as we trust in Jesus, whose death, burial, and resurrection prove God's plan to be trustworthy and his power to be sufficient to perform his eternal will.

Because God is so good and so great, there is no way to predict what God will bring to pass in your life. But the gospel promise of Jesus is yours now and forever. And the good news is sufficient to enable you to live with expectant joy. If sorrow were able to gain entrance into heaven it would be there only as we reflect on our lack of faith in God while on earth. Teana and I have learned this and as a result have also learned to place our hope in God alone. But one day we will stand in heaven, awed by God's plan, speechless at his goodness, rejoicing in eternal fellowship, and bowing before the God who grants us "a beautiful headdress instead of ashes, the oil of gladness instead of mourning, the garment of praise instead of a faint spirit . . . that he may be glorified" (Isaiah 61:3).

Until then,

His purposes will ripen fast,
Unfolding every hour;
The bud may have a bitter taste,
But sweet will be the flower.

(William Cowper,
"God Moves in a Mysterious Way")

Personal Application Projects

1. Read Psalm 139:1–18.
   (a) What do these verses teach about God: his omniscience and omnipotence?
   (b) What do these verses tell you about God's work in a child's life?
   (c) What do these verses reveal about God's plan for you and your children?
   (d) Take the time right now to tell God that you are trusting him with the life of your child or children.
2. Read Isaiah 53.
   (a) Which verses evidence God's redemptive plan through the suffering of Jesus?
   (b) What does this tell you about God and suffering in your own life?
   (c) Now read Hebrews 4:15–16 and contemplate what this tells you about Jesus.
   (d) In response, spend time before God's throne in prayer.

3. Read Psalm 46.
    (a) What fears do you possess in connection with the loss of a child?
    (b) What does God promise to be to you?
    (c) How can you apply these truths to your present circumstance?
    (d) Be still before God and think on his "works" toward you.

4. Read Psalm 16:1–2, 5–9, 11.
    (a) What does the psalmist mean when he says "I have no good apart from you" (v. 1)?
    (b) What does verse 9 say is the result of employing verses 5–8?
    (c) What benefits do we possess in making God our refuge (v. 1)?
    (d) Have you made the Lord your refuge? Consider memorizing verse 11 to remind you of that blessing.

5. Read Romans 11:33–36.
    (a) What is the writer so amazed about in verse 33?
    (b) What are the answers to the questions of verses 34 and 35?

(c) Why does the apostle glorify God in verse 36?

(d) Is this your confession? What keeps you from trusting God so that you can glorify him for what has transpired in your life?

6. Read Matthew 11:28–30.

   (a) What does Jesus promise in these verses?

   (b) To whom is Jesus offering this promise?

   (c) Have you accepted his invitation? If not, will you?

   (d) If you haven't done so already, confess your need for Christ and ask him to be your Savior.

7. Consider which statements in this book have made the greatest impact on you. Write down a few of them in a notebook or journal.

8. Write a list of the Scripture verses that were meaningful to you and then circle those that you intend to memorize to transform your mind and strengthen your heart.

9. Read 2 Corinthians 1:3–4. If you were going to tell someone how God has spoken to you, blessed you, or changed your life in the midst of your heartache, what would you say? Write

down a few key thoughts, important phrases, or particular Bible verses to share.

10. Read Romans 8:28-30.
    (a) What are the divine links in the golden chain of salvation?
    (b) How does this knowledge build the confidence that Paul expresses in verse 28?
    (c) Consider committing these three verses to memory.

11. In times of grief, we are sometimes tempted to go it alone. Be sure to stay actively connected to your church family. If you are not part of a church that faithfully teaches the Bible, consider reading HELP! I Need a Church, which is part of this same mini-book series.

Where Can I Get More Help?

If you have any questions about anything in this mini-book, or want to discuss God's amazing grace, please email me at reggieweems@gmail.com.

In addition to the books I have already recommended, Teana and I discovered real encouragement in the perspectives of theologians and pastors.

James W. Bruce III, *From Grief to Glory: Spiritual Journeys of Mourning Parents* (Scotland: Banner of Truth Trust, 2008)

Gloria Furman, *Labor with Hope: Gospel Meditations on Pregnancy, Childbirth, and Motherhood* (Wheaton, IL: Crossway, 2019)

Nancy Guthrie, *Holding on to Hope: A Pathway through Suffering to the Heart of God* (Carol Stream, IL: Tyndale Momentum, 2015)

John MacArthur, *Safe in the Arms of God: Truth from Heaven about the Death of a Child* (Nashville: Nelson, 2003)

Ronald H. Nash, *When a Baby Dies: Answers to Comfort Grieving Parents (Grand Rapids: Zondervan, 1999)*

Matt Perman, What Happens to Infants Who Die? (https://www.desiringgod.org/articles/what-happens-to-infants-who-die)

Paul Tautges, *A Small Book for the Hurting Heart: Meditations on Loss, Grief, and Healing* (Greensboro, NC: New Growth Press, 2020)

Endnotes

1 Samuel Rutherford, Letters of Samuel Rutherford (Carlisle: Banner of Truth, 1973), 14.

2 In this chapter it will be necessary to discuss some of the physical elements involved in losing a child, but my hope is to do so with sensitivity.

3 Of course, this statement exempts the Lord Jesus, who, in his incarnation, was simultaneously, wholly, and perfectly divine and human. By virtue of that divine/human perfection and his sinless conception, birth, life, death, and resurrection, he perfectly secured our salvation (2 Corinthians 5:21).

4 John McArthur, Safe in the Arms of God: Truth from Heaven about the Death of a Child (Nashville: Nelson, 2003), 89–90.

5 George M. Marsden, Jonathan Edwards: A Life (New Haven: Yale University Press, 2003), 27.

6 John Newton, The Works of John Newton (New Haven: Nathan Whiting, 1824), 347.

7 C. S. Lewis, The Weight of Glory and Other Addresses (New York: Harper Collins, 1949; 2001 edn.), 26.

8 Charles H. Spurgeon, "Infant Salvation," preached September 29, 1861. In Metropolitan Tabernacle Pulpit (London, 1861), 505.

9 Samuel Rutherford, A Selection from His Letters, from Christian Classics Ethereal Library, at: ccel.org/ccel/rutherford/letters.html; accessed 4/20/2010.

Books in the Help! series include...

- Help! Disability Pressures Our Marriage
- Help! He's Struggling with Pornography
- Help! I Can't Forgive
- Help! I Can't Get Motivated
- Help! I Can't Handle All These Trials
- Help! I Feel Ashamed
- Help! I Have Breast Cancer
- Help! I Need a Church
- Help! I Want to Change
- Help! I Want to Model Submission in Marriage
- Help! I'm a Single Mom
- Help! I'm a Slave to Food
- Help! I'm Anxious
- Help! I'm Being Deployed
- Help! I'm Confused About Dating
- Help! I'm Depressed
- Help! I'm Drowning in Debt
- Help! I'm In a Conflict
- Help! I'm In A Painful Marriage
- Help! I'm Living With Terminal Illness
- Help! I'm So Lonely
- Help! I've Been Traumatized by Combat
- Help! My Anger is Out of Control
- Help! My Friend is Suicidal
- Help! My Grandchild Has A Disability
- Help! My Kids Are Viewing Pornography
- Help! My Parents Abused Me When I Was A Kid
- Help! My Spouse Has Been Unfaithful
- Help! My Teen is Rebellious
- Help! My Teen Struggles With Same-Sex Attractions
- Help! My Toddler Rules the House
- Help! She's Struggling With Pornography
- Help! Someone I Love Has Alzheimer's
- Help! Someone I Love Has Been Abused
- Help! Someone I Love Has Cancer

More titles in preparation

For current listing go to:
https://www.shepherdpress.com/store/lifeline/

About Shepherd Press Publications

» They are gospel driven.

» They are heart focused.

» They are life changing.

Our Invitation to You

We passionately believe that what we are publishing can be of benefit to you, your family, your friends, and your work colleagues. So we are inviting you to join our online mailing list so that we may reach out to you with news about our latest and forthcoming publications, and with special offers.

Visit:

www.shepherdpress.com/newsletter

and provide your name and email address.